The State They're In
young people in Britain today

Brigid McConville

YOUTH·WORK·PRESS

5

07

Y O U T H · W O R K · P R E S S 2008

11 JUN 2008

Published by

17–23 Albion Street, Leicester LE1 6GD.
Tel: 0116.285.6789. Fax: 0116.247.1043.
E-Mail: nya@nya.org.uk
Internet: http//www.nya.org.uk

ISBN 0 86155 195 8

£8.50

© November 1998

Y O U T H • W O R K • P R E S S
is a publishing imprint of the National Youth Agency

Contents

Preface

THE STATE THEY'RE IN takes stock of key issues affecting young people as we approach the new millennium. What are the challenges and difficulties they face during the crucial time of transition into adulthood? And what should be our priorities in supporting them at this stage?

This book explores a range of topics, including the major issues of education and employment, identity and behaviour, health and wellbeing. This represents a broad sweep, but in our view it is essential to pay attention to all aspects of the lives of young people rather than concentrating on particular features of behaviour, especially those which are perceived as problems.

There are, it is true, many young people with particular needs, and some of these will be addressed within the *In from the Margins* conference on 2 November 1998, at which this book is launched. Nonetheless, we will not be able to understand those 'on the margins' unless we pay attention to the experiences of all young people, and it is with this aim that this book has been written.

Our three organisations – the National Youth Agency, The Prince's Trust and the Trust for the Study of Adolescence – either work with, or represent the needs of, young people who are excluded or marginalised from mainstream society. In our different ways we are committed to finding ways to assist such young people to overcome disadvantage and to be successful in their family, employment and social lives. We are aware of many inspiring initiatives in progress, a selection of which is outlined in this book. Nonetheless, there is a long way to go before every young person has access to such initiatives, and we very much hope to see these examples move from the local context to become widespread good practice.

The government is putting in place a range of measures to address the difficulties that our young people face. We welcome the introduction of such measures, while at the same time emphasising the necessity for coherent local and national planning so that there is a greater coordination of services at all levels. There still remains a high level of ignorance concerning the experiences of young people, and there is a real need for this problem to be addressed.

Perhaps the present government might

consider instituting a regular review of the circumstances of young people? An annual 'State of the Young Nation' would be of enormous benefit to all who work for and with this group. The planning of services for young people cannot take place unless it is underpinned by good quality information. It is our hope that this publication, in association with the conference *In From The Margins*, will raise awareness, and will give professionals and policy makers an insight into the worlds of young people in Britain today.

John Coleman, Trust for the Study of Adolescence
Arwyn Thomas, The Prince's Trust
Tom Wylie, National Youth Agency

Chapter One – A Time of Transition

What it is to be young

THE NOTION of youth as a 'time of transition' is widely discussed among youth researchers and policy makers today. There is a concurrent argument that youth is actually a time not just of one but of many transitions – into adulthood, into the labour market or alternatively into long-term unemployment and social exclusion. So what, in practice, are young people going through as they pass from childhood into their teens and then adulthood?

One particular facet of growing up today which has enormous implications for the experiences of young people and for society is that youth lasts much longer than it did in the past, starting earlier and ending later.

Before they even leave primary school, children are subject to influences which have previously been regarded as suitable only for teenagers or adults. Through the media they hear about contraception and abortion, violence and drugs, relationships, music, fashion and popular culture.

The children of today are often sexually aware far sooner than were their own parents, while health educators have been arguing that drugs awareness programmes should begin in the first years of primary school. Physically too, young people are maturing sooner with puberty starting on average three years before it did a century ago.

Adolescence not only starts earlier; it goes on for longer. In the past, most young people were considered to have reached adulthood within a few years of leaving school when they would get a job, get married and start their own family. But today's young people stay in school or further or higher education for much longer than past generations. They live at home with their families of origin for longer too.

Even when young people do leave home for a job, a college course or a new relationship, they are more likely to return when the course, job or romance ends. Many young people today will leave home not once, but many times in succession before they finally achieve independence.

Another way in which the distinctions between adulthood and childhood have become blurred is through the delay in financial independence which many experience. Having consumer power is one of the markers of an adult in our society, but with longer years in education coupled with the collapse in the youth job market, young people tend to be dependent on their parents – entirely or in part – until well into their 20s.

Even when young people do find jobs, the chronic housing shortage of recent years means that there aren't enough houses or flats available. Many have no option but to stay at home until they have saved enough to enter the housing market.

When does a child become an adult?

There is more ambiguity surrounding the transition to adulthood than in the past. Young women today may have become mothers – but not yet have left school. Young men may be old enough to get married, drive a car, vote – but they can't get a job or afford to leave their parents' home.

Young people can:

- work part-time at 14;
- leave school and go into full-time work at 16;
- vote at 18; and
- claim full social security benefits at 25.

'When I was younger, 18 seemed like – wow, so grown up! But now I am 18 – and I don't feel like an adult at all.' Andy, 18.

'It's a gradual process. It's about experience and taking responsibility. I know people of my age who seem much older, and that's because they work, whereas I'm still a student.' Clare, 17.

'I rely on my family's support totally. I couldn't do my A-levels or go to university without them.' Zoe, 18.

Another very significant factor in stretching out the time of transition to adulthood is the great increase in numbers of those staying on in education or training up to the age of 18. As jobs have become more difficult to obtain, qualifications have become more desirable, and significantly more teenagers and young adults are going on to university.

Sources of support

SO WHAT help is there for young people as they try to negotiate their own route through this complicated and vulnerable time of transition? Firstly, the family has a crucial role to play in supporting teenagers and young adults. Eighty per cent of 11 to 16-year-olds surveyed by The Industrial Society (*2020 Vision Summary Report*) said that they feel a sense of belonging to their family, while 79 per cent of 16 to 25-year-olds said the same.

Parents can and do get closely involved with their teenagers' education by helping with homework, encouraging study, building confidence and aspirations, and by liaising with teaching staff. Families also have a vital role to play in providing emotional support at times when young people may be struggling with difficult issues of identity, self-esteem and sexuality.

Many young people do look to their parents for guidance and information about the adult world, from how to behave at work to thorny matters of personal relationships. Even teenagers who seem to shun their parents – especially in the company of their peers – will turn to them for help and reassurance in times of crisis.

Friends are another vital source of support, solace – and fun – for young people. Eighty-six per cent of 11 to 16-year-olds and 85 per cent of 16 to 25-year-olds say they feel a sense of belonging to their group of friends (*2020 Vision Summary Report*) – which suggests that young people feel that friends are even more important to them than family. To know other young people, to share in social events and to help each other in times of trouble; all these aspects of belonging to a peer group are central to young people's sense of worth.

Schools and colleges are also a potential source of support. Apart from their more conventional teaching role, there is great scope for personal encouragement and counselling from teaching staff – as well as from trained counselling staff. Group activities at school or college, such as sport and drama, can also help young people develop their confidence, self-knowledge and social skills.

For those who may be struggling with their own personal transition to adulthood, a wide range of youth organisations now exists to support young people and extend their abilities and opportunities. In addition, many schools and youth organisations now have mentoring schemes, in which adults from the local community establish supportive friendships with young people, advising them and encouraging them through sensitive times.

The number of telephone helplines available to young people in distress has also mushroomed in the last decade. There are now helplines for young people who feel lonely or depressed, who need advice about health or time to talk about their sexuality. Best known of all perhaps is ChildLine which takes many thousands of calls every year from children and young people who have suffered mental, physical and/or sexual abuse.

A wide range of youth counselling services across the country also provides

Fig 1 – Numbers living in the parental home, by age and gender, 1991

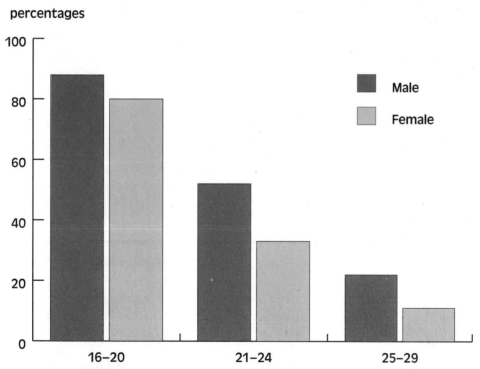

From: *Key Data on Adolescence*, Coleman J. Trust for the Study of Adolescence (1997)
Source: Heath and Dale (1994)

vital support, while the mental health organisations, concerned by the steep rise in young men's suicides, are increasingly arguing the case for young people.

Last but not least, the local community – including neighbours, adult friends and extended family members – can be a crucial source of help to young people in transition. In this context they can learn to make adult friendships, tap into networks of support and information – and form long-term bonds of affection and respect which will stand them in good stead well into the future.

Vulnerable young people

GIVEN THAT the family is expected to be a major source of support to young people today – and for longer than in past generations – it follows that those who have experienced family difficulties and/or breakdown are likely to be at a serious disadvantage.

Yet these days families' resources are often stretched by unemployment, or looking after elderly relatives, or the costs of divorce. Family life has changed immensely and today's teenagers are far more likely to grow up in families where parents are divorced, have remarried or have never been married.

Many more young people than before are growing up in single parent households. This can sometimes mean poverty for children, and often the absence of a positive male role model. If only one parent is at home, young people may miss out on the other parent's network of relatives who can potentially give them a

not all young people.

'leg-up' into adult life – such as help or contacts in finding that crucial first job.

The rise in homelessness among young people has been linked to conflict in the family, especially rows with step-parents. Young people can find themselves homeless because they have left their family home after an argument – but they don't yet earn enough to pay for their own

Community? Whose community?

This generation keenly feels an absence of community. According to the Industrial Society's *2020 Vision Summary Report*, only around one in five of all young people feel part of their local community or neighbourhood.

Karen is 17 and lives in a small West Country town: 'Where I live, it's not a community. The children in my street all go to different schools around town chosen by their parents. Later on they move away because there is nothing in this area apart from one factory and the nuclear power station. And because we are better educated, we want more. Even the immediate family is splitting up. There is no duty left; people don't feel so loyal. My mum grew up with her own mother just down the road, but now she is always complaining that my sisters – who have left home – never phone.'

Meanwhile, resources for young people have been steadily eroded over the past 20 years. There have been reductions in wages, benefits and grants for young people. Despite rising needs for youth provision, services have been cut.

'The overall balance sheet points strongly to a declining share in resources,' argues the Carnegie Young People Initiative's document, *Years of Decision*. 'There seems to be a disturbing shift of attitude towards young people where their positive achievements are often taken for granted or derided as not really counting ... Instead the focus is on young people's negative contributions, offending behaviour, drug taking, etc. Youth is defined as a problem.'

place. However, homeless young people don't generally want to leave home; they are mostly forced out by family tensions, made worse by poverty.

Those young people who are entirely without family support — like many of those leaving care homes — face particular stresses and difficulties in finding their feet. A high proportion of those who are homeless are young people leaving care homes. According to *The Carnegie Young People Initiative: Years of Decision*, we have cause for concern about 'the poor educational outcomes, high risks of unemployment, homelessness or poor quality of jobs on leaving care, as well as the unmet emotional and psychological needs of young people in care … More recently there have been concerns about young women entering the sex trade from care.'

Young disabled people also face additional difficulties in negotiating jobs, training, relationships and independence. They suffer discrimination not only through negative attitudes to their disabilities but through lack of access to many services and facilities. For many, the transition from intensive children's special needs services to the adult world leaves them vulnerable and isolated.

Young people from ethnic minorities face a level of discrimination in education, in employment and in the wider society that often puts them at a serious disadvantage. Racial harrassment and violence are a daily threat to many young people from ethnic minorities across the country.

Research published by the Office for Standards in Education has shown that African-Caribbean pupils are between three and six times more likely to be excluded from school than their white counterparts. Levels of unemployment among young African-Caribbean men are twice those of white men, while the numbers of reported deaths of black young people in police custody is another cause for concern.

There is also a widespread — and false — perception in our society that young men from ethnic minorities are more likely to be criminals. In fact, some evidence shows very little difference between the levels of property crime in white and African-Caribbean communities, while Pakistani, Bangladeshi and Indian young people show lower levels of all types of offending.

The widespread problem of mental ill health in young people is both a symptom and a cause of vulnerability. Psychiatric disorders are the largest cause of illness among young people, while suicide is the second most common cause of death among young men. Up to 20 per cent of teenage girls are thought to suffer from depression, while there are some 70,000 girls and young women in the UK who suffer from anorexia nervosa.

The reasons for these high rates of mental health problems are not established, but one theory is that young people are more likely to be dependent upon alcohol and drugs. Young people who grow up in families where a parent has an addiction problem are especially at risk as they strive towards independence and adulthood.

Living in a disadvantaged area can also make a tremendous difference to a young person's chances of making a successful transition to adulthood. Recent decades have seen a widening of the gap between rich and poor in different parts of the country and within cities and towns. More and more low income families are now concentrated within socially disadvantaged council estates, with little hope of escape.

In short, young people more than any other group are vulnerable to social and economic forces which have caused disruption, unemployment, poverty and homelessness not only in this country, but across the world. Meanwhile the social networks which once helped to absorb the impact of change can no longer be relied upon. It is a mistake to assume that – when in difficulties – young people can turn to their families or communities for support.

> ### Key facts
> - There are seven million teenagers in Britain today. Of these, 3.6 million are between the ages of 10 and 14, while 3.4 million are between the ages of 15 and 19.
> - The last 30 years has seen a rise in the divorce rate across the West, together with a rise in the numbers of people living together and having children outside of marriage.
> - The number of couple families with dependent children (up to aged 16) has decreased from 91.4 per cent to 77.5 per cent between 1971 and 1994. In the same period, lone parent families increased from 8.6 per cent to 22 per cent of all families.
> - Over a million under 16-year-olds are living in stepfamilies, while a further million-and-a-half are in stepfamilies for some of their time.
> - In 1995, between 200,000 and 300,000 young people in Britain experienced homelessness.

Key challenges: identity, independence and intimacy

ON THE personal level too, young people face particular challenges as they enter their teens and embark on the long and often difficult transition to adulthood. Along the way they will strive to establish a sense of individual identity through emotional as well as financial independence from family.

With the advent of the teenage years, many of the certainties of childhood are over. Family and home cease to be the hub of existence. Parents' opinions and values are daily being challenged by those of peers and other adults. Young people are learning that there are other explanations for the world, other versions of the truth, other systems of politics, religion and culture.

These are the years in which young people ask themselves 'who am I?', 'why am I here?' and 'what is it all about?' It is a time during which they may try to come to terms with what it means to be male or female, black or white, heterosexual or homosexual.

Adolescence is a time when many young people fall in love and have their first sexual experiences. Often these are shortlived, but it is a steep learning curve with the joys of intimacy closely linked to the risks and emotional pain of rejection.

And while all this is going on young people are edging towards autonomy. At times they want nothing to do with their parents; nothing could be more embarrassing, especially in front of their friends! At other times they desperately need a mum or dad to be there for them and take them back into the comfort and security of the home. In the long-term they will need to find a way of balancing family and friends, of being their own person while still keeping in touch with family.

Sometimes this emotional and psychological transition to adulthood can be quite straightforward, but for some young people it is agonising. In a relatively stable family home there is usually space and security to explore these issues and to let off emotional steam in comparative safety.

Often young people like to turn to adults other than their parents – neighbours, older friends, relatives – to help them work things out, especially in times of conflict with their own parents. Friends, teachers, youth workers, mentors, health services, peer education projects, telephone helplines – all have a part to play in helping young people through.

Those without supportive family and neighbourhood networks, however, are more vulnerable to confusion and distress, and less likely to develop the confidence and self-esteem they will need to take their place as fully participating citizens in society.

Agenda for action

- **Housing legislation should recognise that 16 to 17-year-olds – particularly those leaving care and those in rented accommodation – are a priority group.**
- **An equitable benefits system for people under 25.**
- **More 'intermediate' housing, such as Foyers and YM/WCAs.**
- **Young people should have the opportunity to develop both their social and practical skills with the help of an adviser or mentor.**
- **A minimum wage for young people and a legal responsibility on employers to support their training.**

Chapter Two – Getting On: Education and Employment

Changes in education

THE PAST decade has seen extensive changes in education, training and employment for young people. The days have gone when young people could confidently expect to go from school into a job, perhaps with a few years of college in between, and since the collapse in the youth labour market it has become much more difficult for young people to get a good start in life.

However, realising that better qualifications make it easier to get a job, young people have been working hard to improve their opportunities. This generation has more qualifications than ever before, at higher grades, while young people today spend more time than ever in education and training.

Ten years ago, 26 per cent of young people in England of the GCSE year group gained five or more A–C grades. By 1995 that figure had risen to 45 per cent, with girls doing better than boys. At A–level too, exam performances improved, with young women again doing better than young men. (Despite much debate about

whether examiners have been setting lower targets, the leap in performance rates is too great to be dismissed as grade inflation.) In the same period, the numbers of young people over 16 staying on in education has risen by a quarter.

Meanwhile, there have been major changes in the direction and organisation of education.

Management changes such as the introduction of grant maintained status led to one in five secondary schools opting out of local authority control. Whether or not this has improved performance in those schools has not been established.

National league tables for schools have also been introduced. These have put immense pressure on certain schools especially in disadvantaged areas where the added value a school brings to its pupils cannot be measured by this single yardstick of academic achievement.

It's likely too that league tables have put schools under pressure to enter as many pupils as possible for exams, whether their chances of success are good or not.

Another important innovation is the national curriculum. While many have welcomed its clear academic focus, there have been voices raised in protest that it puts too many restrictions on other important subjects and life skills. Teachers now have less time than ever for personal and social education (PSE) – including the vital topic of sex education.

The government has recently stated its commitment to teaching not three, but four Rs – the fourth being relationships – but this has yet to find its way into an overcrowded academic curriculum.

What young people want from education

- practical, relevant life skills and qualifications;
- an environment in which they want to learn, in which educators boost young people's confidence and enthusiasm;
- teachers who are well trained, committed and who have time to teach;
- more resources, i.e. smaller classes, more equipment and books, more facilities for young people with particular needs;
- a wider curriculum with less limited subjects;
- an alternative to streaming which can stigmatise and demotivate;
- more financial support and encouragement to go on to further and higher education;
- more liaison between schools, colleges and employers;
- freedom from discrimination and bullying; and
- good careers advice, counselling and support.

(Source: *2020 Vision Summary Report*. The Industrial Society, 1997)

Another major change, which is arguably linked to the introduction of league tables, has been the dramatic rise in both temporary and permanent school exclusions since 1990, particularly in disadvantaged inner-city areas.

The numbers of children excluded from school went up four times between 1990 and 1995 – 84 per cent of these were from secondary schools, mostly in years 10 and 11. Up to six times as many black pupils as white pupils face exclusion. Boys are four times more likely as girls to be excluded.

The fact that two out of three young people who are permanently excluded from secondary school never return to full-time mainstream education has enormous implications not just for the futures of those who are excluded but for society as a whole. Exclusion, together with poor attendance, means that young people are likely to gain few qualifications which in turn damages their employment prospects.

At the same time, disaffected young people who have been excluded from school are more likely to get into trouble. Forty-two per cent of offenders of school age who are sentenced in the Youth Court have been excluded from school.

The steady squeeze on resources for education has also taken its toll not only on teachers, school buildings and facilities, but on the most basic requirements – such as books. According to the 1997 Ofsted *Annual Report*, shortages in books and equipment affect teaching adversely in one in four secondary schools and one in ten primary schools.

This situation has had a negative effect not just on the morale of teaching staff, but on young people who cannot fail to take on board the messages sent by shabby school buildings and overstretched facilities.

Politicians claim that the education of young people is a priority: young people have yet to see the evidence.

The great gender debate

SINCE THE introduction of the national curriculum, boys and girls have had equal access to all subjects taught in school. Yet gender still affects the educational performance of school pupils from an early age. Girls start to achieve better results than boys in English from the age of 7 and by the time they are 16, girls are more successful than boys at every level in GCSE.

In England in 1995, 49 per cent of girls aged 16 had five or more A–C grades GCSEs compared with 40 per cent of boys. (Comparable figures for Wales are 46 per cent and 36 per cent.) Girls have traditionally done well in English and foreign languages, but girls now also outperform boys in science, maths and technology at GCSE. Meanwhile, the numbers of 16 to 18-year-olds staying on in full-time education has increased by a quarter over the past decade, with more young women (74 per cent) than young men (68 per cent) choosing to continue their studies.

At A-level, the gender gap continues with girls turning away from maths and science, subjects which could lead them into careers in engineering and technology. Far more young men than women are taking maths, physics and technology, while more young women than men study English, foreign languages and social studies. Geography, economics and computer studies are becoming increasingly male dominated. Broadly speaking, these patterns continue at undergraduate level.

In 1975 there were some 80,000 women and 160,000 men at universities or polytechnics. By contrast, in 1995 there were over 400,000 women and over 400,000 men who were full-time undergraduates in England and Wales. Drop-out rates are high, however.

When it comes to vocational qualifications (such as NVQs, GNVQs, RSA, City and Guilds and BTEC), young men gain more awards and at a higher level than young women. The gap is particularly marked in crafts and related occupations. Gender stereotypes persist in apprenticeships too where young women are concentrated in the caring occupations, hairdressing and business administration while young men predominate in industries such as engineering, manufacturing, construction and the motor industry.

There has been widespread concern about the relatively poor academic performance of boys especially at secondary school level. Not only are girls scoring higher in exam terms, but they have fewer behavioural problems in school, they are more conscientious about doing their homework and they are more likely to cooperate with teachers by bringing the correct equipment to lessons and responding to teachers' comments about their work.

The Chief Inspector of Schools, Chris Woodhead, has called for secondary schools to 'make every effort to combat an anti-achievement culture among boys which can develop in Key Stage 3 (the early years of secondary school), alienating some boys from all academic work'. Ofsted's *Annual Report* links boys' relatively poor performance to weaknesses in basic skills and a lack of commitment to school, but notes that so far, the gap between boys and girls shows no signs of narrowing.

Some educators have argued for single

sex schools as one way to help pupils achieve their potential, but as yet there is no conclusive research to say that single sex schools are more successful than mixed schools. There are relatively few single sex schools and they often have other features – such as selection procedures – which set them apart from the mainstream.

On the margins

WHILE MANY more young people are staying on longer in education and gaining more qualifications, an increasing minority find themselves on the margins of education. One in 16 pupils leaves school each year without any qualifications and with little hope of making it into a decent job.

Some young people choose not to go to school or college because they don't see any point in it and/or rebel against the rules. For many, the roots of social exclusion lie in primary education, in that boys and girls who lack the basic skills to cope with secondary school are likely to be disruptive and to truant. Yet 20 per cent of pupils arrive at secondary school with reading ages well below their chronological age.

Bullying is also a major problem for young people, and a survey for the Association of Lecturers and Teachers (April 1998) revealed that 300,000 pupils have stayed away from school because of threats of violence. Black and Asian young people face a particularly high level of racist bullying. Other young people leave education sooner than they would like because they can't afford to stay on in college, or haven't got the confidence to go on. Still others have to take care of children or other relatives.

Of those who are supposed to be in school, a staggering one in ten plays truant. This is a problem which has snowballed during the last 20 years, now involving many younger children. More than half-a-million pupils a day are involved in truancy, while some 80,000 children hardly ever turn up to classes at all. According to the police, these are the young people who get involved in drugs and petty crime, causing problems across the board.

Study support

'We all come because we want to – no one makes us. The older kids come to help – no one makes them either.'

This is what one student at the CAESAR study support centre at the Collegiate High School in Blackpool has to say about the project. The centre – which has a relaxed and welcoming environment – uses peer supporters (helpers of the same age) to address problems of literacy among some of its young people.

The centre is open to students, parents and members of the community at lunchtimes, after school and some evenings. Up to 80 students choose to attend for a range of activities. Twice a week, extra teaching staff come to the centre to support students in basic skills work.

So far, results have been encouraging and nearly three-quarters of the pupils given additional support in reading have made better than expected gains in their reading levels.

'I think Study Support is different from lessons,' said one pupil, 'because it is more relaxed and more enjoyable. There is no teacher forcing you to do what they want and there is relatively large freedom of choice of activities.'

Boys are far more likely than girls to find themselves on the margins of education. Four times as many boys as girls are excluded from school and boys are nine times more likely to be disruptive or show disturbing behaviour. Disruptive pupils in turn affect their classmates: over a third of pupils say that they have problems at school due to disruption by others.

A disproportionately high number of those excluded are young people in care and those from African-Caribbean and traveller families. (Of traveller children, nearly two-thirds – some 10,000 – of secondary school age, are not registered at any school.) Pupils with emotional and behavioural problems and those with lower reading attainment are also more likely to be excluded from school.

At the root of many of these problems is the strong and persistent link between low standards in education and socio-economic disadvantage. Many schools are serving disadvantaged inner-city areas or outlying estates, or they are in small towns hit by unemployment and decline. In schools with over 40 per cent of pupils eligible for free school meals, only 20 per cent of pupils get five A–C GCSEs compared with the national average of 43 per cent.

After exclusion, young people's education is continued in local authority controlled Pupil Referral Units. There are over three hundred PRUs in England which aim to reintegrate young people into mainstream education or training, or prepare them for work. However, Ofsted has found that standards in PRUs are generally too low, even when the educational history of pupils is taken into account, and that the teaching in PRUs makes little impact on the low levels of pupils' literacy and spoken language.

On a positive note, however, Ofsted also found that pupils' behaviour and attitude to education often improves as a result of the small groups and good relationships with teachers in PRUs.

One in five pupils is likely to experience learning difficulties at some stage of their school career (according to the *Warnock Report*, 1978), with the risk of finding themselves on the margins of education. Of those pupils with a statement of special educational needs (i.e. with learning difficulties arising from intellectual, sensory, physical or emotional disability), 54 per cent are being taught in mainstream schools today. But the recent changes in organisation of SEN provision have left many LEAs with serious gaps in provision, training and resources.

Of pupils in specials schools for those with a wide range of disabilities, Ofsted inspectors found that 'pupils make good progress in about a quarter of special schools, but there is substantial underachievement in one in six' (Ofsted *Annual Report*, 1997).

Another group of young people who have been largely failed by the education system are those who have been in local authority care. These children who face many disadvantages in life, have often had to cope with difficult, insecure and/or abusive experiences. Many have had to change schools often and without warning.

Educational achievements and qualifications are crucial to the future of these young people, and yet according to Ofsted *The Education of Children who are Looked After by Local Authorities* 'national concern that children who are being cared for by local authorities are under achieving in schools has existed for some time … (their) educational needs are not clearly understood or accorded sufficient importance by teachers, social workers and carers'.

Ofsted concludes that 'coordinated action by education and social services agencies to raise the children's achievements is urgently required if the children are to be able to overcome the difficulties which they face in childhood and be well equipped to lead productive adult lives'.

From young people's perspective

According to *2020 Vision Summary Report*, The Industrial Society (1997):

'Schools and colleges are seen by young people as largely successful in providing academic knowledge, but are regarded by many as failing to teach the practical, life and social skills that young people see as important. The majority (63 per cent) of 16 to 25-year-olds believe that schools do not prepare people for life in the real world. However, many are optimistic that ... current problems in education could be solved if more resources were provided to reduce class sizes and improve teacher quality.'

Of young people (16 to 25) surveyed by the Industrial Society about their education:

- 63 per cent felt that school does not prepare them for the real world;
- over a third said they have problems at school due to disruptive pupils; and
- one-third said school is boring.

Employment and unemployment

WHEN IT comes to paid work, young people are eager for good opportunities. Eighty per cent work or have worked in some sort of job, although these are mostly low paid and casual. Most see work as a vital part of life, and object strongly to the media stereotype of 'workshy' young people.

Their prevailing view is that people should work – and some even argue that people who refuse to work should lose their state benefits. For many, work provides not only an identity, but a meaning to life. Paid work helps young people feel that they belong to society.

Yet in today's fiercely competitive job market few young people can leave school and go straight into a decent job and youth unemployment has become a major concern. Over the past two decades the numbers of jobs available to school leavers – especially unskilled jobs – has plummeted. (Only 7 per cent of 16 to 17-year-olds today have jobs, compared with 61 per cent 20 years ago.)

What young people (16 to 25) say about work

- decent pay is important (61 per cent);
- getting on well with colleagues makes a job enjoyable (67 per cent);
- only half expect to be in permanent employment with the same or consecutive employers;
- a job which benefits society or helps others is more enjoyable (28 per cent); and
- lack of respect and lack of recognition at work are the main negative aspects.

In addition, young people from ethnic minorities face severe problems of racism in finding employment. A report commissioned by the National Youth Agency (1997) found that young people from ethnic minorities are twice as likely to be unemployed as their white counterparts. A panel of representatives from ethnic communities writing in the NYA's magazine *Young People Now* suggested that racial discrimination against African and Caribbean young people, institutionalised racism – in the fields not only of employment, education and training, but in social and welfare provision and criminal justice – is a permanent blight on the lives of young people.

Historically, black and Asian people who came to Britain in the '40s and '50s settled in cheap housing which was often in inner-city areas. Decades on, these areas have suffered from lack of investment and they don't offer the opportunities found in other more affluent areas. Education is often poorer and job options are strictly limited.

The effects of racism are felt not only on the institutional level, but on the personal level. Institutional racism can prevent young people gaining access to jobs, training and education, but racism on a personal level can destroy confidence and self-esteem – 79 per cent of black Caribbean girls and boys, and 70 per cent of Asian boys and girls are bullied at school. Six out of ten black people and four out of ten Asians suffer physical or verbal abuse because of the colour of their skin, while 65 per cent of young people aged 16 to 25 believe that not enough is being done to combat the effects of racism.

Being without work and without money is a depressing and frustrating experience which can leave young people without an anchor in their lives. Yet they are caught in a Catch 22 situation: they know they can't get jobs without experience – but can't get experience without jobs. Not surprisingly, many have come to believe – from their own experience and that of their parents – that the lack of adequately paid work today is a major social problem.

The New Deal

Young people have enormous potential and energy, but in many communities they are given few chances to achieve success. Youth unemployment is now recognised as one of the biggest challenges facing our society.

The government has responded with the New Deal initiative, intended to help young people break into the world of employment. At the beginning of this year (1998), over 16,000 young people took part in the launch of the government's New Deal in Pathfinder areas across the country. Young people aged 18 to 24 who have been unemployed for six months or more are eligible to join the New Deal which begins with a Gateway programme – an initial intensive course of advice and guidance. Those who don't move off welfare and into work within the first six months then have a range of options including work placements, further education and training, working for a voluntary organisation and starting their own business.

It is too early to gauge the success or

The Fork Lift Truck Driving project

The Fork Lift Truck Driving project, in the deprived area of Blaenau in Gwent, Wales, has enabled all the young men who participated in it to escape long-term unemployment. Each one gained a license and was hired as a fork lift truck driver within months of the project. On the basis of this success, The Prince's Trust-Action's South Wales Committee organised a second project.

It was Youth Choices, a local group which works to get young disadvantaged people into training or work opportunities, who originally identified the need for fork lift truck driving skills in the area. But when they were unable to raise the necessary funds, The Prince's Trust stepped in with a £960 grant for the first project as well as meeting the expenses of the second project.

failure of the New Deal. Critics argue that six months is not long enough in which to address deeply entrenched problems, and that private sector employers will cream off the best job candidates, leaving the voluntary sector schemes as 'sink' options.

Some young people are also understandably suspicious – given past experience – that this may be yet another scheme to get them off the dole.

According to the Unemployment Unit and Youthaid, much hinges on the \economy: if there is a downturn – as some predict – private sector employers may not be able to come up with the 30,000 job vacancies needed (at six-month intervals) for New Deal jobs.

Yet there is great interest throughout the country in making the New Deal work. To a large extent, the future of the next generation depends upon it.

Making changes

SO WHAT can be done to encourage young people back into education and ultimately, employment? When children were asked (by the trade unions UNISON and NASWE) why they truanted, they blamed:

- boredom in class;
- favouritism by teachers; and
- the early start to the school day.

A recent report (NYA/NIACE) identifies various key elements – including individual attention, fun, opportunities to develop skills and relevance to the world of work – which can motivate young people to get back to learning. To young people whose experience of school has meant boredom, humiliation and failure, these aspects are vital if they are to achieve and progress.

Another crucial element in motivating young people is choice. When young people vote with their feet, coming in to youth centres or homework clubs, they can often achieve what they failed to do at school – because they want to.

The Prince's Trust promotes and provides funding for over five hundred Study Support centres in schools and youth organisations that serve some of the most disadvantaged areas of the country, raising standards and tackling numeracy and literacy problems, involving the business community and parents and making effective use of summer school programmes.

Study Support aims to narrow the divide between the 'haves' and the 'have nots' in education by targeting resources into areas of need. It can produce an increase of between 10 and 15 per cent in the number of young people achieving grades A–C at GCSE or equivalent. Out-of-school hours learning, pioneered and developed by The Prince's Trust over the last six years, is an important element of *Excellence in Schools*, the 1997 government policy document on education.

Agenda for action

Education

A shift in emphasis

- The national curriculum should be less subject-dominated and more relevant to the daily lives of young people.
- Teachers need to adopt a wider range of teaching methods to involve young people in active learning as problem solvers, rather than imparting received wisdom.
- More PSE, sex education and pastoral work so that pupils can know themselves and their community.
- Attention to beliefs, attitudes and values, as much as skills, knowledge and understanding.
- Recognise that many young people find school boring and school rules arbitrary. These pupils need more individual attention – increasingly difficult for hard pressed teachers to give.
- More education for parenthood.

A change in provision

- More choice of home or community-based provision for young people who don't like school.
- More community schools with facilities for after school activities, homework clubs and family learning workshops.
- More linking/bridging courses between school and FE colleges.

Employment

- Action to end racial discrimination in employment.
- There should be a minimum wage for young people and a legal responsibility on employers to support their training.
- There should be a confidential hotline for young people to report exploitative employers or poor training providers.
- Personal development plans and/or mentors for young people.
- Broad community education for young people, especially in disadvantaged communities, where there would be coaches in the arts, sports, outdoor and environmental education and information technology.

Chapter Three – Sex and Sexual Health

Our sexualised society

OF ALL the social changes of the past 30 years, among the most significant and far-reaching concern sex and sexuality. In the space of a generation, women's lives have been changed dramatically by the availability of contraception and abortion, homosexual and lesbian rights have become a major political issue and the stigma of living 'in sin' and/or having an illegitimate child has virtually disappeared.

Today we live in what appears to be a much freer society. Images of sex and of (mostly female) nudity abound, in magazines, newspapers, film, television and advertising. This is the Wonderbra age in which sex sells everything from cars to ice cream. Frequently these sexual images feature young people. As a result young people are becoming sexually aware much earlier than they once did.

Not surprisingly, this sexualisation of society has had its impact on young people's sexual behaviour and they are becoming sexually active earlier than in the past. According to the National Survey of Sexual Attitudes and Lifestyles (NSSAL),

women who are now in their '60s lost their virginity on average (median) at age 21. For today's young people, however, the median age of first intercourse is 17. (These figures differ according to ethnic background; young Asians are less likely [24 per cent] to have had sexual intercourse by age 17 than their white [53 per cent] and African-Caribbean [51 per cent] peers.)

Other types of sexual activity start early too. The age at which young people today report their first experience of sexual intimacy is 14 for girls and 13 for boys. Health Education Authority research shows that 46 per cent of 16-year-olds, 61 per cent of 17-year-olds and 78 per cent of 19-year-olds have had sex or been sexually active with another person.

Young people today also reach physical maturity at an early age. The age of first menstruation has dropped by approximately three to four months per decade during this century. In the 1860s, the (mean) age of menarche was over 16; today it is just over 13.

Meanwhile, significant changes in health and medical care have affected young people's sexual behaviour. Different types of contraception have become more easily available while terminations are easier to obtain for young women. The advent of HIV/AIDS has added a new dimension of risk to sex, while sexually transmitted infections are also on the increase among young people.

In some important ways, however, social attitudes have not caught up with these rapid changes. On the one hand, commercial and media images appear to encourage young people to be sexually active. On the other, our tabloid press periodically whips up a new moral panic about underage sex or schoolgirl mums, teenage abortion or young people's clinics.

Young people find themselves faced with some confusing and damaging double standards: sex is the modern holy grail – but when young people 'do it', it's bad. News and views about sex are constantly being broadcast on every channel – yet there are certain things about sex which young people are not supposed to know. The consequence is that instead of getting the information and support they need to make safe and satisfying choices about sex, all too often young people encounter a baffling brick wall.

Teenage pregnancy

THESE DOUBLE standards about sex have had an impact on Britain's teenage pregnancy rate which is now the highest in Western Europe. Many European countries have teenage conception rates less than half those of England and Wales.

The rate of conception in 1995 in England was 8.5 per 1,000 among under 16-year-olds and 58.7 per 1,000 among 16 to 19-year-olds. Between 50 and 90 per cent of teenage pregnancies are unintended and more than half of girls under 16 end up having abortions, while a third of the older age group also have abortions. One of the targets of the government's Health of the Nation initiative in 1991 was to reduce pregnancy rates among the under-16s by half, yet the latest figures (1996) show them at their highest since 1990.

The factors which influence teenage conceptions are complex, but age is one important factor. Young people who start having sexual intercourse before the age of 16 are the least likely to use contraception. Research shows that 50 per cent of young women having intercourse before the age of 16 do not use contraception, compared with 33 per cent of those aged 18 or over. In general, the younger teenagers are when they start having intercourse, the less likely they are to use contraception.

This is partly because of ignorance about how to use contraceptives correctly or consistently. Young people – especially young teenagers – may lack the confidence to ask for advice about contraception and

---

What young people really feel about having sex

- Loving relationships are seen by most young people (86 per cent) as 'very important' or 'important' when people have sex.
- The reasons that young people give for having sex for the first time include being in love, curiosity, 'natural follow on' and peer pressure.
- Girls are more likely to feel pressured by their boyfriends, while young men are twice as likely as young women to feel pressured by their friends.
- More than half of young women who had sex before the age of 16 later regretted it.

(Sources: Sex Education Forum and the Sexual Life Styles study).

to make the best use of the services available. Fear of the unknown combined with anxiety about confidentiality may put young people off visiting their local clinic. Again, low self-esteem or poorly developed negotiating skills can make it very difficult for a young girl to insist on her boyfriend using a condom – or vice versa.

Ready or not

Emma is 15. Confused, isolated, afraid ... and pregnant. Now what?

If it's difficult for many adults to admit their fears and worries about sex, it can be that much harder for many young people with less experience and confidence. Not surprisingly, teachers can find it quite a challenge to start off a discussion about sexual issues. A useful way to break the ice is through creative presentations in drama and dance.

An innovative piece of dance theatre called Ready or Not, by the tred theatre company from Barnsley, takes an honest look at Emma's situation, teenage pregnancy and what it means from both male and female perspectives. Young people have found it entertaining, imaginative and fun.

The dance piece, which is aimed at those aged 12 and over, has been performed in schools and community centres. It can be followed by discussion and workshops, based on an informative and stimulating support pack.

Barnsley pupils said: 'The workshop was my favourite. I had more fun than I thought,' and 'When can we do it again!?'

Poor access to family planning services has also been blamed for the high teenage abortion rate in the UK compared with other European countries. In a 1994 survey organised by the Brook Advisory Centres, 44 per cent of requests from teenagers who were asking for either emergency contraception, or the pill or free condoms (from the NHS) failed to get an appointment within a week. In the same exercise, on 12 per cent of occasions teenagers were refused any help or put off by the attitude of the staff.

Our society's repressive attitude towards young people's sexuality also means that they are not getting as much clear or accurate information about sex as they would like. In spite of the prevailing myth that informing young people about sex leads them to experiment, the opposite is true. When young people do get good sex education – at home and at school – they are more likely to postpone starting a sexual relationship.

Social disadvantage is another important factor in teenage pregnancy. Generally speaking, young women who live in deprived areas are more likely to get pregnant and to have babies at an early age. In turn, children of teenage parents who grow up in relative poverty are more likely to experience family conflict, low educational attainment, poor health – and to have children of their own when they are young.

Young people need not only accurate information and accessible services, they need confidence and self-esteem to take charge of their sexuality. Emotionally damaged young people may seek sex and babies as a way of filling a deep emotional void. On the other hand, the higher the motivation and aspirations of young women, the more likely they are to want to take control of their lives.

Disadvantaged young people and those who are discriminated against are more likely to have problems of low self-esteem. They are also more likely to have early and unhappy sexual experiences. Vulnerable young people, like those in the care system, may have had painful life experiences which leave them with low self-esteem and lacking in the skills and confidence to say 'no' to unwanted sex. Young people who have been in care are far more likely than others to become parents at an early age, and to work in the sex industry.

In short, our high teenage pregnancy rate spells continuing disadvantage for many, because teenage pregnancy is not only a symptom of poor education, unemployment and social exclusion, but it often perpetuates them too.

Young people and contraception

THE MAJORITY of young people who are sexually active do use contraception, however. A 1996 survey by the HEA found that 86 per cent of young men and 91 per cent of young women (aged 16 to 19) used contraception when they first had intercourse, mainly the condom and the pill. Six per cent subsequently used emergency contraceptives. In another HEA study, less than one in ten young people said they had not used contraceptives the last time they had intercourse.

The same survey asked young people aged 16 to 24 what contraceptive method they used the last time they had intercourse: half of them said the pill, while 43 per cent said the condom. The latest General Household Survey shows that condoms are growing in popularity among 16 and 17-year-olds.

Those times when young people do have unprotected sex are likely to be after drinking alcohol. More than half of teenagers say they are less likely to use condoms after drinking. Unprotected sex is also more likely to happen when young people are not in a steady relationship.

> **Modern myths**
>
> It's not true:
>
> - That 'when young people have plenty of information about sex, together with contraception and abortion, they are more likely to experiment with sex'. In fact, the reverse is true.
> - That 'boys are only interested in one thing'. In fact, while it is more difficult for boys to talk about their feelings, they are very interested in sex education which is suited to their needs.
> - That 'young people can be persuaded to be gay or lesbian'. Individual sexuality is determined by factors far deeper than argument or information.

Taking risks: HIV, AIDs and STDs

PUBLIC AWARENESS of HIV and AIDS has taken a great leap forward in the past decade and young people today clearly share in that awareness. Exactly what impact this has had on their sexual behaviour is difficult to assess, but most teenagers today who are in sexual relationships have a steady boyfriend or girlfriend. (This doesn't necessarily mean they are monogamous however; research shows that a quarter of those who say they are in steady relationships also have sexual partners outside that relationship.)

Meanwhile health educators believe that the safer sex message has been received and understood by most young people today, while condoms are now standard equipment in their social lives. According to the HEA's 1997 health update *Sexual Health*, most young people today are well informed about safer sex (those of higher economic status are better informed), although most would welcome more and better information. The vast majority of young people (95 per cent) surveyed by the 1995 Health Education Monitoring Survey agreed or strongly agreed that 'using condoms would show that someone was a responsible person', while 62 per cent said they would always use a condom with a new partner.

News stories about new combined drug treatments which are now available for HIV/AIDS have recently muddied the picture however, causing a certain amount of public confusion over the difference between treatment and cure. More than 10 per cent of 16 to 24-year-olds surveyed by the HEA in 1997 said that knowledge of new treatments means they would worry less about becoming infected with HIV in a new sexual relationship.

Sexually transmitted diseases (STDs) other than HIV/AIDS are, however, on the increase and young people are less well informed about the risks. STDs are a major cause of ill health in Britain and can have long-term consequences including infertility, ectopic pregnancy and genital cancers.

Research at teenage clinics shows that the rates of most STDs among young people are higher than the national average. Young women in particular suffer from STDs, especially in the 16 to 19 age group when they have much higher rates of infection than their male contemporaries. This is a worrying gender gap which suggests we need improved health education strategies aimed at young men.

Fig 2 – Number of new cases seen in NHS genito-urinary medicine clinics in England, 1992

Condition	Males			Females		
	under 16	16–19	All ages	under 16	16–19	all ages
Infectious syphilis	0	4	228	3	15	110
Post-pubertal uncomplicated gonorrhoea	43	834	7691	116	1370	4401
Post-pubertal uncomplicated chlamydia	27	1235	13089	271	4209	15309
Herpes simplex – first attack	17	331	6140	72	1333	7877
Wart virus infection – first attack	94	2226	27169	340	6269	23955

From: *Key Data on Adolescence*, Coleman, J. Trust for the Study of Adolescence (1997)
Source: Department of Health. KC60 returns. Quoted in '*On the State of Public Health*'. (1993)

Boys' talk

AS THE figures on page 23 show, all is not equal when it comes to issues of sexual health, and in recent years awareness has been growing that boys and young men have particular needs which must be addressed.

Boys generally are less well informed about sex than girls. Not only do parents tend to focus their concerns upon their daughters rather than their sons, but fewer boys than girls get information from GPs or sexual health clinics – because they are less likely to go there in the first place.

In the school environment too, peer pressure can encourage boys to act macho and mess about during sex education sessions. The problem is compounded by the fact that sex education in schools usually focuses on reproduction and biology, leaving young men further marginalised.

As a result, boys learn much of what they do know about sex from their male friends and from pornography. It is often difficult for them to question what they learn because to admit ignorance or inexperience of sex means they haven't yet 'become a man'.

Yet it is vital that we help young men to acknowledge and communicate their feelings and to make responsible choices about contraception and relationships.

Much depends upon it, not just in terms of reducing teen pregnancies and STDs/HIV infections, but in terms of the health and happiness of young men themselves.

Targeting boys and young men

A community project throughout Rhondda Cynon Taf and Merthyr Tydfil is offering boys and young men the opportunity to explore sexuality, sexual health and relationships.

In informal groups run by trained volunteers from the local community, young men (mostly aged 14 to 18) meet to discuss a range of issues from self-esteem and relationships, to contraception, HIV and AIDS and fatherhood. Through games, quizzes and discussions, young people are encouraged to participate and explore their values.

The project, called Healthy Sexuality in the Community; targeting boys and young men, aims to help young men make positive informed choices about their lives.

'Time and again young men report that the best thing about the sessions is that we do not tell them what we think they should know,' says Simon Blake, project officer for the Family Planning Association in Wales.

'We value their experience and we listen to what they want. This means the topics – such as pornography, condom use and fatherhood – are of real interest to them. We build a respectful relationship that is the most useful resource for working with young men. The work is sometimes challenging, often rewarding – and young men's humour and energy is a delight.'

The young men's verdict:
- 'It is really useful to know the signs of sexually transmitted infections.'
- 'I thought I'd be embarrassed but I wasn't.'
- 'I really enjoyed it.'
- 'It was a really good laugh.'

Sex education

SO HOW can we help our young people to make responsible, well informed choices for themselves about their sexuality and sexual health? How can we help them to enjoy their sex lives without the burden of unwanted pregnancy or infection? Above all, research shows that young people want more information about their bodies, sexuality and sex – but from reliable sources like their parents and teachers, as opposed to their friends.

Unfortunately, in this country there is an abiding myth that information about sex encourages young people to try it out. In fact the opposite is true: the more that young people know about sex and the better their access to contraception, the less likely they are to experiment with sex at an early age. According to the National Children's Bureau, a major comparative study of 37 developed countries found that those with greater availability of sex education and birth control for young people also have the lowest rates of teenage pregnancy, abortion and childbearing.

Research shows that school-based sex education can be effective in reducing teenage pregnancies and sexually transmitted infections – particularly when it is linked to local contraceptive services. Many schools try their best to provide young people with good sex education, but they feel frustrated in their efforts by the pressures on teaching time and, nationally, provision is patchy and often inadequate.

Since the 1993 Education Act, the biological aspects of sex education have been made compulsory at secondary schools – but many teachers rarely get past these physical facts. Those other vitally important aspects of sex – such as relationships, contraception, sexually transmitted diseases and so on – may be ignored by schools altogether.

The provision of good quality personal and social education – including sex education – is now an important element of the government's plans for excellence in schools. Schools minister Estelle Morris (Parliamentary Under Secretary of State for School Standards) has stressed the importance of not just the traditional three Rs, but of the fourth R – 'relationships', or emotional literacy.

At the heart of many new initiatives in sex education is the conviction that we must broaden the scope of sex education to include more than the basic physical facts about sex, empowering young people to take responsibility for their own sexual health. Peer education, in which young people are trained to go into schools or other centres to give information to their peers about sex and sexual health, is increasingly seen as an important part of sex education. While peer education should not be used to replace sex education provided by teachers, it can have an

---

Young people's worries

At middle school:

- I'm worried about my periods;
- I worry about boys touching me;
- I am very worried that I'll die when I have a baby;
- I am worried about people making fun of my body;
- I'm very worried about telling my mum I have started my periods;
- Being a dad;
- Gettings AIDS;
- People calling me names;
- Being gay; and
- I worry about whether it hurts when you have sex.

At secondary school:

- Being made to do things I don't want to do;
- That my body is not normal, that everyone else is having sex and I am not;
- What will happen if I do a wee when having sex?; and
- Knowing when a girl wants or doesn't want sex.

Source: Gascoigne, M. (1997) *Sex Education in Hertfordshire Schools* (ongoing research for the Institute of Education). Sex Education Forum NCB.

especially powerful impact.

Parents can also help their children towards safe and responsible decisions by talking openly and honestly about sex. In families where sex is discussed, children are more likely to wait until they are over 16, but in families which disapprove of sex or won't talk about it, young people often start having sex earlier. And as we have seen, young people who have sex before they are 16 are less likely than others to use contraception.

The way forward

THE EMERGING consensus is that sex education and sexual health services for young people must be improved and made easily accessible if we are to lower the teenage pregnancy rate and enable young people to make well informed and responsible decisions.

Young people themselves often say that sex education is 'too little, too late'. They want the opportunity for discussion about relationships. Sex education, they feel, should come either from well trained teachers or from outside experts who are knowledgeable and not embarrassed by the subject.

Agenda for action

- **Drop-in clinics for young people in school, or near school, which cover every aspect of good health and self-esteem, from spots to smoking to contraception.**
- **Information leaflets in school.**
- **Clear, easily accessible sex education and contraceptive advice.**
- **Programmes of education for particular groups such as young gay men and certain ethnic minority groups.**
- **Open access services for sexually transmitted infections.**
- **Better links between school sex education and locally available services for young people – for instance, young people should visit local services as part of their school sex education programme.**

Chapter Four – Young People and Crime

Public perceptions: the wrong end of the stick?

IN THE past 15 years, few subjects have attracted more media attention and public anger than the crimes committed by young people, especially young men. According to the Audit Commission Report *Misspent Youth* (1996), an estimated seven million offences are committed each year by young men under the age of 18. Apart from the personal trauma these cause, youth crime costs the country over £1 billion per year, and the victims between £2 and £3 million.

As a consequence, public fears about young people's behaviour have spiralled, together with demands for ever stronger measures against young offenders, while political leaders have proclaimed themselves not only tough on crime, but tough on the causes of crime.

Since the 1980s, governments have been introducing more punitive sentencing measures. One attempt to reign in the anti-social behaviour of young people came in the form of Boot Camps, supposedly designed to give young offenders a short sharp shock. More recently we have seen the 1994 Criminal Justice and Public Order Act, which introduced an equally controversial sentencing power, the secure training order, to detain persistent young offenders aged 12 to 14.

Youth crime remains a key priority for the current Labour government and the Crime and Disorder Bill (before Parliament at the time of writing, April 1998) contains proposals such as local curfews on children and a new parenting order. The latter requires the parents of young offenders, truants and young people subject to an anti-social behaviour order to attend counselling or guidance sessions.

Yet the widespread public perception that we are experiencing an epidemic of youth crime does not square with the facts. It is true that young people under 21 are responsible for half of recorded crimes, and young men these days are taking longer to grow out of criminal activity. However, there is little evidence of any great increase in the level of crime committed by young men in the past ten years. Crimes committed by young women (who are

Fig 3 – Offences recorded as homicide per million population, by gender and age of victim, England and Wales, 1995

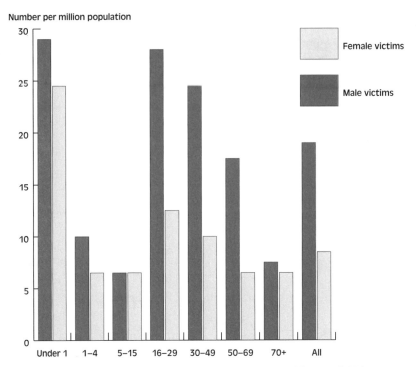

From: *Key Data on Adolescence*, Coleman, J. **Trust for the Study of Adolescence** (1997)
Source: *Criminal Statistics, England and Wales, 1995*. HMSO, London (1996)

responsible for only 20 per cent of youth crime) have increased, but only to a limited extent.

There has also been strong criticism of many of the harsher initiatives taken by government, mostly on the basis that they don't work. The Penal Affairs Consortium has described the secure training order as 'a retrograde and damaging measure which will increase rather than reduce offending by young people and which represents an indefensible misuse of public expenditure'. The same body condemned the emphasis on fining parents as 'likely to produce injustice, to place struggling families under even greater stress and to increase ... the problems which promote delinquency,' while describing the short sharp shock

detention centres of the early 1980s as 'the most clear cut failure in recent British penal policy'.

And while there is little evidence of any great increase in the level of crime committed by young men in the past decade, there has been an increase in the numbers of young adults and children in prison. According to *Young Prisoners; A Thematic Review* by HM Chief Inspector of Prisons (1997), 10,954 young people under 22 were in prison service custody in June 1997, a 6 per cent increase from the figure for January of that year.

In this same period, the numbers of children under 18 in custody rose by 11 per cent. HM Chief Inspector of Prisons predicts further rises in these figures while

The State They're In

Fig 4 – Persons found guilty of, or cautioned for, indictable offences per 100,000 population by age group, 1985–95

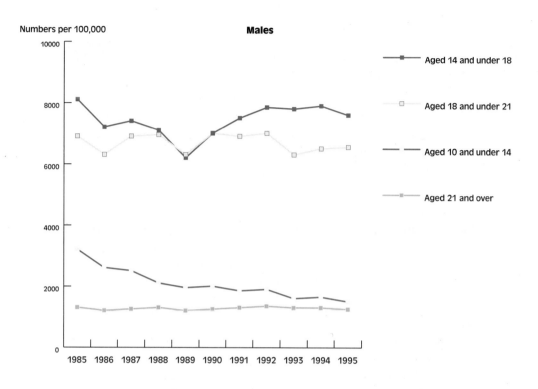

Numbers per 100,000

Males

Aged 14 and under 18
Aged 18 and under 21
Aged 10 and under 14
Aged 21 and over

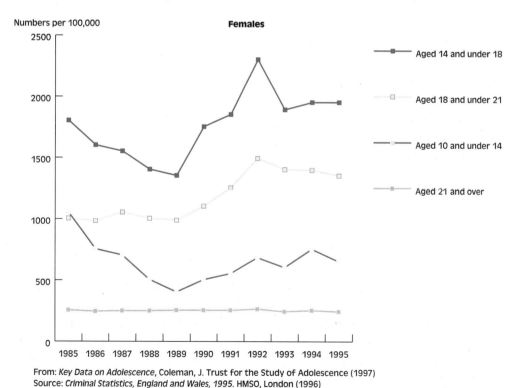

Numbers per 100,000

Females

Aged 14 and under 18
Aged 18 and under 21
Aged 10 and under 14
Aged 21 and over

From: *Key Data on Adolescence*, Coleman, J. Trust for the Study of Adolescence (1997)
Source: *Criminal Statistics, England and Wales, 1995*. HMSO, London (1996)

Home Office projections suggest that by March 1999 there could be 3,100 remanded and 8,600 sentenced young male prisoners – including children – in custody.

Gender and crime

THE TERMS 'youth crime' and 'young offenders' mask very significant differences between males and females in this arena, reflecting the differences in gender roles in society as a whole. Young men and young women have markedly different patterns of offending, not only in terms of how – and how much – they offend, but at what age they do so.

While offending by young women is rare, young men are responsible for approximately 80 per cent of all crime committed by those under 21. For young men, offending behaviour rises steadily from the age of 10 to peak at 18. For young women, the peak age of offending comes earlier at aged 14, reflecting the fact that young women mature earlier. By the time they are teenagers, young women are committing a quarter as many crimes as young men (self-reported rates). By the time they are in their 20s, this figure is down to a tenth of the male crime rate.

Young women not only offend less and earlier than young men, but their offences are generally less serious and less dangerous. Unlike young men, young women are less involved in macho street culture and more involved with family and children. According to research into the prison population (*Young Prisoners; A Thematic Review*), the most common crime committed by young men is burglary. Other frequently committed offences are theft and robbery.

Young women by contrast tend to have less extensive criminal histories, with convictions mostly for shoplifting and other thefts. Young women are also less likely to commit those crimes most feared by the public, including mugging, rape, assault and burglary. Yet while young women are still in the minority of those who commit crimes, their numbers are growing – as are the numbers of women in prison which have increased by 60 per cent in the past five years.

There are similarities too between young men and young women offenders, mostly in terms of emotional damage and material deprivation suffered in childhood. Seventeen per cent of young men in prison admitted to having suffered abuse of a violent, sexual or emotional nature (this is probably an underestimate given the difficulties men have admitting abuse). Nearly three times as many (49 per cent) young women have suffered abuse.

The potential for breaking the cycle of abuse by education in parenthood is highlighted by the fact that (according to *Young Prisoners; A Thematic Review*) almost a quarter of young men in prisons are fathers or expectant fathers, while more than half of young women in custody have dependent children or are pregnant.

The lives of young women especially – and their needs in prison – are profoundly affected by the fact that so many of them are mothers, often at an early age. Many women, even while they are in custody, bear a lot of responsibility for their children.

A high proportion of young women in prison have also experienced poverty, low educational attainment, family breakdown and abuse. Around half have been in care, often subject to extremes of distress and disruption. Young women in prison are far more likely than other women to have been assaulted or raped. A disproportionate number are from ethnic minority groups.

The Trust for the Study of Adolescence argues that many young women should not be in prison at all, and that those who are should be in specialist prisons with staff trained to understand the difficulties of women in custody.

Why do they do it?

THE QUESTION of why young people become involved in crime is as contentious as any other in this field, with a major ideological tussle currently taking place between those who point the finger at individual moral laxity and those who emphasise the social and emotional deprivation suffered by many young offenders.

Young people who revealed their own reasons for offending behaviour to the Audit Commission Report *Misspent Youth*, put family or friends at the top of the list, followed by 'no money', 'alcohol/drugs' and 'nothing to do'.

Other studies have blamed:

- a low level of teenage supervision in the neighbourhood;
- lack of constructive leisure activities for teenagers;
- not being in school;
- having friends involved in crime; and
- living in a rundown neighbourhood.

According to *Young Prisoners; A Thematic Review*, 'the main reason given for young people's criminal behaviour was involvement with drink and/or drugs'. This research revealed that almost a quarter of

Fig 5 – Reasons given by young offenders for their behaviour

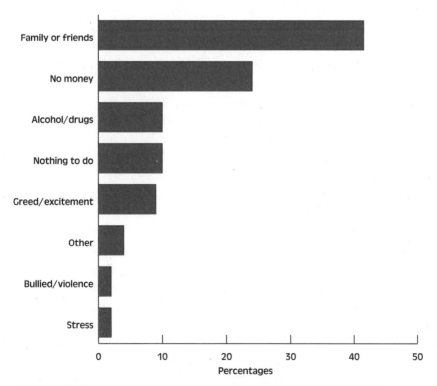

From: *Key Data on Adolescence*, Coleman, J. Trust for the Study of Adolescence (1997)
Source: *Misspent Youth: Young People and Crime*. Audit Commission, London (1996)

...ng male prisoners said they had been under the influence of alcohol at the time of the offence, while up to a quarter claimed a past or current drinking problem. Mental health is also a serious problem for young offenders. Over 50 per cent of young prisoners on remand and 30 per cent of sentenced young offenders have a diagnosable mental disorder.

In terms of social factors, most young offenders come from disrupted home backgrounds with over half of under 18s in custody having a history of care or social services contact (compared with 2 per cent of the general population). Many have also been failed by our education system, over half having been excluded from school. Only a small minority of young people in prison have any educational qualifications.

Children and young people who kill or commit other violent crimes are often known as Section 53 offenders (as they are sentenced under this section of the 1933 Children and Young Persons Act). *Violent Victims*, Dr Gwyneth Boswell's study of abuse and loss in the lives of Section 53 offenders (commissioned by The Prince's Trust), found that 72 per cent of the 200 young people surveyed had experienced emotional, sexual, physical or organised/ritual abuse, or combinations of these; 57 per cent of the sample had also experienced significant loss in terms of a bereavement or loss of contact with someone important to them – and in some cases, both.

'In only 18 out of 200 cases studied were there no recorded or personally reported evidences of abuse and/or loss,' according to the report. 'The total number who had experienced both phenomena was 35 per cent, suggesting that the prevalence of a double childhood trauma may be a potent factor in the backgrounds of violent offenders.'

> ### Empowering young people
> The Youth Empowerment Project (YEP) in Calderdale, Halifax (supported by The Prince's Trust) helps young people from three housing estates to develop social and personal skills to make informed choices about their lifestyles and careers. Instead of hanging out on the streets with nothing to do, young people are offered alternatives in the form of workshops, outings, drugs education and nights out.
>
> 'It's made me grow up,' said Lisa, aged 16. 'Before coming here I used to vandalise but now I don't. I used to have a really bad attitude to the police but now I know they're here to help and not to kill your fun.'

Young people as victims of crime

WE HEAR a great deal about young people as criminals, but far less high profile is the issue of young people as victims of crime. Young men in particular are at the sharp end of street violence. Young men (aged 16 to 29) have the highest risk of being murdered, mugged or otherwise attacked. Not surprisingly, nearly a quarter of young men and nearly a half of young women aged 16 to 24 feel unsafe walking alone after dark.

Young people from ethnic minorities as well as gay young people experience a high level of discrimination which often manifests itself in violence. More than 61 per cent of gay men and lesbians under 18 have been harrassed, while 48 per cent have experienced a violent attack, according to HEA figures.

Arguably, many young women involved in prostitution are both victims and perpetrators of crime. Girls who run away from home because of conflict with parents are at high risk not only of becoming offenders, but they may get involved in prostitution after adults have introduced them to drugs. At least 5,000 children under 16 are used for prostitution in Britain.

What can be done?

ALTHOUGH WE are currently seeing an attempt at synthesis, there are traditionally two responses to youth crime: one focusing on punishment or justice, the other emphasising welfare. The welfare approach argues that troublesome young people are the products of disadvantage, and so the best way to tackle youth crime is to combat poverty and deprivation. For instance, evidence from America shows that when children grow up with the benefits of pre-school education, they are far less likely than others to be involved in crime – and far more likely to earn more money and own their own homes.

A major concern of those who argue against the use of custody for young people is the high rate of reoffending among young people who have received custodial sentences. While 62 per cent of adults re-offend within five years of a custodial sentence, the rate for young people aged 14 to 17 is 90 per cent. Meanwhile, concern is growing about the state of our prisons and their negative impact on many young people.

In contrast, the justice approach sees crime as a matter of personal responsibility and choice, and looks for punishment as a deterrent. While this approach may work for the small minority of people who commit most crimes, its critics say that

---

Young people taking action against crime

Some of the more successful initiatives of recent years have recognised the complexity of the situation and have involved young people in finding strategies to combat crime.

A recent community safety project in Barnsley involved young people in identifying 'what would make Barnsley a better place to live'. The team of research assistants, aged 16 to 25, conducted initial interviews with 200 people. Focus group discussions followed to formulate a comprehensive questionnaire – The Barnsley Young People's Survey – which brought a thousand responses.

The top three concerns voiced by young people in Barnsley were:

- more action to stop crime and burglary;
- tackling the drugs problem; and
- help with finding jobs.

The solutions they suggested included:

- action against racism to protect young people;
- greater respect for young people from the police;
- better and cheaper public transport, especially for those in rural areas;
- that teachers should listen to the views of pupils and obey the same rules;
- revealing bullies and addressing their problems; and
- providing drug users with special counsellors and rehabilitation centres.

The survey not only revealed great diversity among the views of young people, but showed their concern about being victims of crime and about feeling unsafe, undervalued, underpaid and disenfranchised from the decisions which affect them.

---

prison stops young people from maturing into more responsible individuals.

Most young people do grow out of crime, and if in the meantime they can be diverted from offending, much crime can be prevented. Many local schemes, police educational programmes and holiday schemes are successful with this kind of approach.

Projects which alleviate the sense of disaffection felt by many young people, especially in disadvantaged areas, are likely to reduce offending behaviour. In an ideal world that means better education, and more jobs and resources for young people.

The Steering Wheels project

Young offenders and others facing a range of difficulties have the opportunity to gain useful job-related skills while also improving their literacy and numeracy at the Steering Wheels project in Bridgend, Wales.

The project holds workshops in an old garage on an industrial estate, where up to a dozen young people at a time can learn about mechanics, using old vehicles provided by the police. The Prince's Trust South Wales Committee paid for the tools and equipment used in all the training.

Many of the young people involved have a history of interrupted education, and so sessions on health and safety in the workplace double up as a means for developing basic skills which will help them in the rest of their lives. Most of the young people signed up for the workshop in order to get a job, but ended up leaving with much more.

Another major thrust of the campaign against youth crime has been that prevention is cheaper than dealing with its consequences. According to *Young People and Crime in Scotland* (The Prince's Trust – Action, 1997), youth crime now accounts for nearly 40 per cent of total crime in Scotland and costs an estimated £730 million a year, not to mention the psychological distress involved. The average cost of each recorded youth crime is approximately £2,000. By investing in preventative work (for instance, youth work to counter boredom and develop personal and social skills), £1,700 of this would be saved for each crime prevented.

The potential contribution of youth work to crime prevention was highlighted in the 1994 study *Preventative Strategy for Young People in Trouble*, commissioned by ITV Telethon and The Prince's Trust and undertaken by Coopers & Lybrand. The vast majority of youth work does not have crime diversion as an explicit objective, however, the report found 'a large body of subjective evidence which convinces us of a linkage. (This is) strongest for youth work which is carefully targeted at young people "at risk", has clearly defined objectives, offers an intense and long-term process and provides a challenging and educational experience.'

According to the report, the benefit to society of preventing a single youth crime is a cost saving of at least £2,300, as well as immeasurable savings in terms of individual distress and fear. To be cost effective in crime prevention, youth work projects would need to prevent between 1 in 5 and 1 in 14 of 'average' participants from committing one offence in one year. If those young people were known re-offenders, however (committing six offences a year), a youth work project would be cost effective if it diverted between 1 in 22 and 1 in 75 of young people from crime in one year.

Mentoring

In the meantime, youth agencies all over the country are doing effective and innovative work to combat social exclusion and disadvantage. For instance, some are encouraging young people back on track by pairing them with adult mentors from their own community. Mentoring schemes, like the award-winning Dalston Youth Project in East London, can play a significant role in crime prevention. DYP links young people with a trusted adult advisor (mentor) while providing training opportunities and links with local employers.

DYP works with some of the most disadvantaged young people in Hackney, targeting those who have few skills and qualifications. These young people often have few positive adult role models. Many are in care or living with a single parent, having left school early. Volunteer mentors from the community, usually from a similar ethnic background, work one to one with a young person over the course of a year while they also take part in college taster programmes and pre-employment training.

DYP's results have been impressive – 73 per cent of the young participants have gone to college, into training or work, while arrests were reduced by 61 per cent. The Audit Commission's Report, *Misspent Youth,* recommends mentoring schemes such as DYP as effective ways of working with young offenders in the community.

Agenda for action

Strategies for dealing with youth crime need to focus on individuals identified by the youth justice system as well as groups of young people at risk of committing crime. They also need to address young people in general to reduce disaffection.

What works:
- help with finding jobs;
- help with drug and alcohol problems;
- benefits advice;
- training and work experience in supportive environments cuts down on crime;
- cognitive skills training which teaches young offenders to think before they act, to work out alternatives – and to recognise how their crimes affect other people;
- involving young people as partners in community development helps tackle drug problems;
- peer group education in drugs issues (in which young people are trained to raise awareness with their own age group) works better than programmes run by teachers;

- youth work and work in schools which increases confidence, motivation and skills, also diverts young people from crime;
- more money for preventing youth crime. Greater investment in youth work can cut the huge costs of the crime bill;
- neighbourhood mediation services to reduce nuisance or disorderly behaviour by young people; and
- specialist mentoring schemes.

To divert young offenders from repeating crimes:
- strengthen families with parental training, family centres, support groups, help for single parents and step-families;
- reduce school exclusions and truancy;
- reduce drug and alcohol abuse;
- protect young people from association with their delinquent peers;
- support young people in making the transitions to adulthood; and
- young women in custody should have their own specialist units with trained staff.

Chapter Five – Healthy Mind, Healthy Body

YOUNG PEOPLE are, by and large, a healthy lot. Like the rest of the population, they have benefitted from modern health care and improved nutrition, so that today's teenagers are taller and heavier than in previous generations, with puberty starting earlier too. They don't often need medical help, visiting the doctor only two to four times a year, which is less than the average adult.

According to the HEA report *Young People and Health: the health behaviour of school-aged children* (1997), the majority of young people consider themselves to be healthy too, with one in four defining themselves as 'very healthy'. And far from the couch potato stereotype, many of today's young generation keep fit by taking part in a wide range of physical activities from football and tennis to bike riding and jogging.

As for health in the wider sense of mind, body and spirit, the majority are in good shape too. Most young people feel good about their circumstances and are generally realistic about about the challenges they face. They want to take responsibility for themselves and make

things happen. Many are involved in community activities, education, paid work and volunteering.

Of those interviewed for *Young People and Health*, nine out of ten said they felt 'generally happy about their life at present', and one in three felt 'very happy'. While boys rated themselves more positively than girls (as they did in terms of physical health), over half always or often felt confident in themselves.

Yet there are special concerns when it comes to the health of young people. Almost by definition, young people are prone to taking risks and have a sense of being invulnerable to danger. It follows that the teenage years are a time of particular physical dangers with young people suffering a high rate of injury. (See fig 6, page 38.)

Accidents (including injuries, poisoning and traffic accidents) are the chief cause of death among young people, especially young men who are twice as likely as young women to have fatal accidents. What's more, the health divide between people of different incomes and social class means that young people from

Fig 6 – Causes of death, by age, in the UK, 1994

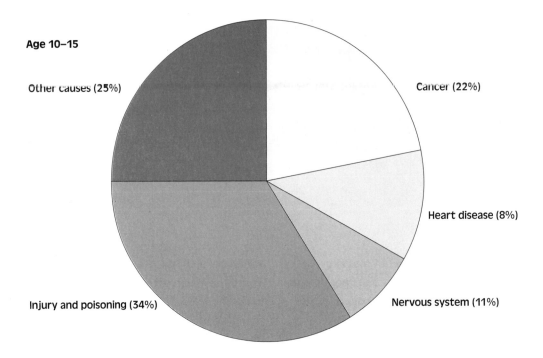

Age 10–15

Other causes (25%)

Cancer (22%)

Heart disease (8%)

Nervous system (11%)

Injury and poisoning (34%)

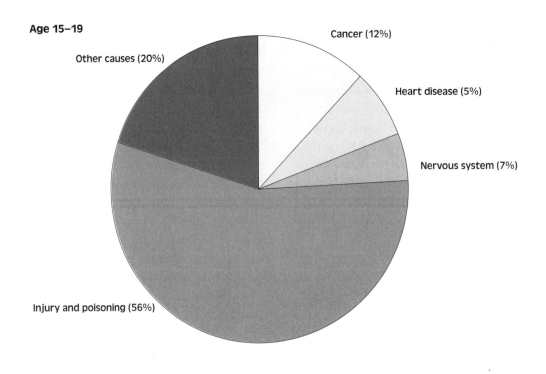

Age 15–19

Cancer (12%)

Other causes (20%)

Heart disease (5%)

Nervous system (7%)

Injury and poisoning (56%)

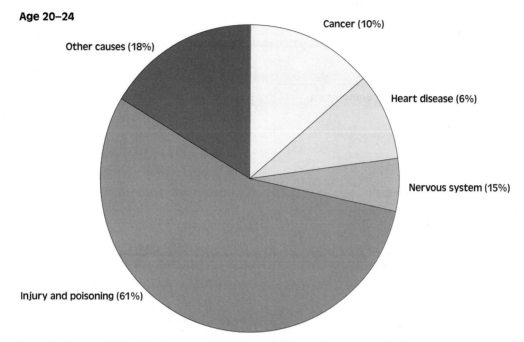

Age 20–24

Cancer (10%)

Other causes (18%)

Heart disease (6%)

Nervous system (15%)

Injury and poisoning (61%)

From: *Key Data on Adolescence*, Coleman, J. Trust for the Study of Adolescence (1997)
Source: *Mortality Statistics*, HMSO, DH2 No.21 (1996)

disadvantaged backgrounds have more accidents than their better off peers. This sense of 'it'll never happen to me' also means that informing young people of the bald facts about smoking for instance, often seems to make little difference to their behaviour.

In recent years too there has been a disturbing rise among young people in rates of smoking, suicide, drug and alcohol abuse, eating disorders, sexually transmitted diseases, respiratory and infectious diseases. Adolescence in particular can be a time of turbulent physical and emotional change, and emotional and mental problems are particularly common in this age group.

Issues like bullying and the social pressure to conform to a slim body shape further pile on the stresses. And as we have seen in Chapter Three, problems of contraception, abortion and teen pregnancy are very much to the fore with this age group.

Many of the factors which affect young people's health are beyond their own control, such as access to doctors and clinics, environmental pollution, access to leisure and sports facilities, food and agriculture policy and, above all, poverty. Poverty undermines health across the whole population and young people are no exception.

Homelessness is especially bad for young people's health, yet national housing policy is often at odds with health policy.

Meanwhile, issues like drug use and HIV infection get most attention from health educators, and while these can have very serious consequences, relatively few young people are affected. This chapter considers not only these problems, but other key health issues for young people – such as mental and emotional illness, smoking, physical fitness and alcohol abuse.

Mental health

THERE IS a worrying gap today between what most young people hope for in life – such as opportunity, stability, equality and tolerance – and what they expect to happen in reality. Many of this current generation are growing up feeling undervalued and excluded. They are well aware that society sees them as a 'problem'; not the best self-image to carry them through this important and vulnerable time of transition to adulthood.

No doubt this sense of exclusion contributes to the fact that psychiatric disorders are the main reason for young people's illness today. While definitions of mental health are always controversial, a quarter of young people are thought to have mental health problems, 7 to 10 per cent of them moderate to severe.

Another factor which can damage a young person's wellbeing is bullying. According to *Young People and Health,* half of all young people are bullied at some time during their school years, while a range of other problems – from racism to unemployment, from family breakdown to abuse – can also put immense pressures on mental health.

For young women especially, the pressure to 'look right' is intense. When asked whether there was any part of their body that they would like to change, 65 per cent of girls in year 11 said there was, compared with 39 per cent of young men (*Young People and Health*). Weight and size/shape are at the top of the agenda when it comes to what girls would like to change and today, 70,000 girls and young women in the UK suffer from anorexia (a rate which is 12 times as high as among boys).

Concern about the mental health of young men on the other hand is increasingly focused on their rising suicide rate. This has almost doubled in the past decade, making suicide the second most common cause of death among young men.

> *'Maybe he was just scared and did not see the point of going on. Maybe he thought it was too much hassle. Maybe he had been thinking about it for so long it all piled on top of him and he just couldn't carry on.'*

Brother of 18-year-old who committed suicide.

Young people and physical fitness

KEEPING FIT is good not just for young people's physical health but for their mental and emotional health too. Exercise relieves stress, improves self image and offers opportunities to have fun and be sociable too. Indeed for many young people, it is the chance to meet with friends which is the strongest motivation for being physically active.

Young people are the most active group in the population, yet research suggests that most are still not taking enough exercise. Ideally, young people should be active (whether that means walking, playing football, swimming or simply running about outside) for about an hour a day

Ulster opportunities

Young people growing up in North and West Belfast, among the most severely disadvantaged areas of Northern Ireland, can face a bleak future. Many leave school without qualifications and without much hope of a job. Teenage pregnancy and drug and alcohol misuse are common.

When a 1992 study of four community-based vocational projects in both Catholic and Protestant areas found that trainees' health and social problems were affecting their attendance, Opportunity Youth (OY) was set up as a holistic personal development and health awareness programme – alongside their vocational training.

OY works to reduce risks to young people's health while improving their chances of employment. Its 300 annual participants are 16 to 18-year-old Jobskills trainees who meet with peer educators (trained young people) in small group sessions for around two hours a week.

OY provides a confidential forum for young people to discuss drugs, sex, alcohol and/or job prospects, as well as information to help them make informed choices about their health. The year-long programme culminates in a residential trip to a watersports centre.

Independent evaluation has shown the dramatic impact of the project on trainees, with teenage pregnancies down by 66 per cent and 70 per cent of drug misusers saying they now want to stop. As one trainee said: 'We discuss things to do with everyday life, like work, drugs, unprotected sex and the risks we've been taking. I've been coming to OY for five months and I've found it useful to talk about the things we never really get the chance to talk about anywhere else, like sexually transmitted diseases and how you could tell if you had one. I've learned a lot about drugs and I don't drink as much as I used to. OY has made me more confident (which) I think will help me with job interviews.'

throughout childhood and their teens. Yet the slowdown in physical activity generally begins at about 6 years of age and continues through the teenage years, with girls doing less than boys.

So, how can we encourage young people to be more active? A range of factors – from the activities of family and friends, to poverty and access to open spaces – make a difference. Young people with active parents tend to follow suit, while the more play spaces children can walk to, the more active the child. Unfortunately, many young people find themselves stuck at home watching television more than they would like to because of parental fears about their safety on the streets.

All too often, inactive girls grow up to be young women who do far less exercise than young men – even though most would like to take more exercise. Only one-third of 16 to 24-year-old young women are active enough to benefit their health according to the HEA, compared with more than half of men of the same age. Young men are more likely to continue to play sports such as football after leaving school, while young women say they lack the time, money or confidence to keep up with physical activity.

Young people and smoking

SMOKING KILLS 100,000 people a year, usually in middle or old age. Yet the damage often starts young. A quarter of 15-year-old boys smoke, while girls are almost twice as likely as boys to be regular smokers once they hit 13. Young people

who smoke generally know about what cigarettes can do to their health, but information alone is not enough to make them want to give up.

And once a smoker, always a smoker – or a smoker who struggled to stop. Addiction to nicotine can be even harder to break than addiction to heroin, which may explain why only 40 per cent of smokers ever manage to break the habit. According to *Young People and Health* the majority of young people (67 per cent) said they started smoking out of curiosity, while 60 per cent of school children who currently smoke would like to give up.

Break free from fags

The image, à la *Trainspotting*, is a filthy mess of money and cigarette butts swirling down a toilet bowl. The logo is 'Smoking makes you SKINT'.

This is just one of the pack of vivid, attention-grabbing cards given out to young people as part of the Break Free Schools Programme, a lively 30-minute presentation for teenagers. The programme was developed by QUIT.

'I have never had so much fun learning about how I am killing myself eight times a day,' commented Laura, aged 15. 'It was light hearted and interesting, but the serious side still shone through. I wasn't aware that as many as 350 people die every day of smoking related illnesses in the UK alone. I'm no longer one of the 10,000,000 smokers who want to quit, but one who has! Thanks!'

Poverty is also an issue when it comes to smoking. QUIT, the national charity that helps people who want to stop smoking, recognises that although better off people are giving up smoking in large numbers, poorer people are not. Smoking rates are particularly high among people who are unemployed, including young adults with families and lone parents.

Pregnancy can also be a stressful time and these days many young people do not have an extended family to support them through it. The Pregnancy Quitline and QUIT's Poverty and Smoking project aim to help smokers under these particular pressures.

Young people and drinking

IN OUR alcohol friendly culture, having a drink is seen as normal and civilised adult behaviour. We blame killjoys for the health warnings while welcoming any evidence that a few glasses of wine are good for us. Naturally enough, young people want to join in the fun. A survey of young people's attitudes (Alcohol Concern, factsheet no. 7) found that:

- 12 to 13-year-olds drink to experience the adult world, to satisfy their curiosity, to start socialising and to say they have tried alcohol.
- 14 to 15-year-olds are testing out their own limits and having fun. They enjoy losing control occasionally, getting drunk and sharing the experience with their friends.
- 16 to 17-year-olds want to show their maturity and experience by drinking more like adults and impressing their girlfriends or boyfriends.

According to the HEA study *Young People, Alcohol and their Social World*, feeling part of a group is central to early drinking experiences. Teenagers don't drink simply because of peer pressure, however; they also enjoy the buzz of alcohol – which has the added advantage of temporarily releasing stress and boosting confidence. This research found that girls often drink

to help them communicate more freely with their friends, while teenage boys saw it as a sign of weakness to refuse a drink.

Snog, Puke, Scrap, Prat

In a novel approach to promoting the HEA's *Too Much Drink? THINK!* campaign, a pair of mime artists known as Fruit Troupe took the campaign's slogans into the refectories of further education colleges in Bristol, Bath and Western-Super-Mare.

Sponsored by the Avon Health Promotion Service, Fruit Troupe used juggling, mime and dance to draw attention to the dangers of drinking too much. Vivid cards with the blunt messages 'Snog', 'Puke', 'Scrap' and 'Prat' were used as props for their act, highlighting some of the consequences of overdoing it.

Quizzes, case studies and newsletters for the students followed, while tutors were encouraged to raise the subject of safer drinking in tutorials.

'I think the cards will have a good effect on boys because they go out to pull,' said Emma, aged 18. 'The cards will make them think about what they are like when they're drunk.'

'When you see the word puke it makes you think what it's actually like, because it is such a horrible word,' said Kate, aged 17.

Meanwhile, there is a lot of money to be made from selling alcohol to young people, and drinks manufacturers and the makers of alcopops are doing their best to exploit the market. Young people are drinking more alcohol than they used to, and drinking it more often. In contrast to smoking, boys drink more than girls of the same age.

By the age of 14, most young people have tried alcohol. By the time they get to 17, many are regular drinkers in bars, pubs and clubs. Binge drinking is also more common among young people. In spite of the law, it's not difficult for under-18s to get hold of alcohol through off-licenses.

The immediate risks of alcohol abuse by young people include accidents, unruly or violent behaviour and unsafe sex. Deaths from alcohol consumption among the under-25s are very few (although drink is implicated in much violent behaviour and many accidents), but as with smoking, the toll taken by heavy drinking shows up later in life.

Young people and drugs

THE DEBATE about drugs has hotted up considerably in recent years. Should cannabis be legalised or not? Should we be locking up drug addicts – or offering treatment? Is America's zero tolerance policy one that we should follow? While the Social Exclusion Unit has been looking at many of the problems often associated with drug taking – such as school exclusion, truancy, rough sleeping and poor housing – the government has appointed a new UK anti-drugs coordinator or Drugs Tsar, Keith Hellawell, who rapidly established these key objectives:

- to reduce the proportion of people under 25 using illegal drugs;
- to reduce the level of reoffending among drug misusing offenders;
- to increase the participation of problem drug misusers, including prisoners, in drug treatment programmes; and
- to reduce the access to drugs among 5 to 16-year-olds.

The issue of drug abuse remains a highly political one, with one national newspaper launching a campaign to legalise cannabis while high-profile figures from pop stars to cabinet ministers find themselves drawn uncomfortably into taking up positions. For unlike alcohol which older people generally think of as a good thing (for themselves at any rate), opinion about illegal drugs usually splits down lines of age.

The older generation tends to think of drugs as an alarming evil. But while many young people do disapprove of drug taking – especially hard drugs – others accept drugs as part and parcel of their culture, especially dance culture. As the magazine *Deluxe* (spring 1998) put it, 'Britain used to have a vibrant music and club culture with a parasitical drug culture attached to it. Now it's the other way around.'

Many young people today believe that 'soft' drugs like cannabis should be legalised and more than half (55 per cent) of 16 to 19-year-olds in England have at some time used drugs (HEA, 1997).

Four out of ten young people in the UK have used cannabis, although far fewer (less than one in ten) has used Ecstasy and

---

Don't trip or you'll fall

Young offenders and students are the main target audience of the drama *Don't Trip or You'll Fall*, which has met with such success that performances have spread from the project's original Buckinghamshire base to Berkshire and Oxfordshire. Over 10,000 14 and 15-year-olds, many from low income and single parent families, have been reached by the play's anti-drug messages.

The drama follows the central character, Ben, through an escalating and painful addiction to drugs. As he progresses from sniffing glue and experimenting with soft drugs at parties to the abuse of hard drugs, Ben's life spirals downwards into stealing, prostitution, emotional chaos, family unhappiness and alienation from his friends.

Don't Trip or You'll Fall has been jointly funded by The Prince's Trust, the Arts Council and local communities.

Fig 7 – Changes over 25 years in responses to questions concerning awareness of drugs

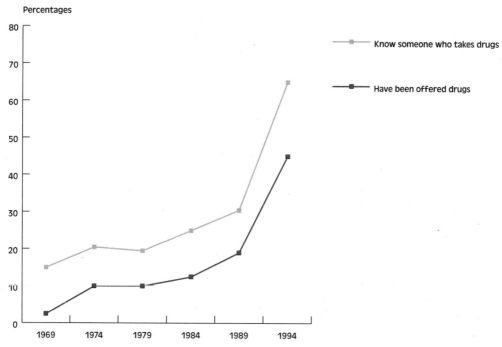

Percentages

Legend:
— Know someone who takes drugs
— Have been offered drugs

From: *Key Data on Adolescence*, Coleman, J. Trust for the Study of Adolescence (1997)
Source: Wright and Pearl (1995)

less than one in a hundred young people has ever used heroin, crack or cocaine. However, illegal drugs are far more widely on offer today than they were 30 years ago.

Drug abuse by young people is linked to a range of serious health problems from life threatening infection to physical injury, from psychiatric problems to the risks of HIV infection. People who inject opiate drugs have a death rate which is 15 times that of non-users.

Illegal drug use is also closely bound up with crime. At least half of all recorded crime has a drug related element while convictions for drug offences in the UK have trebled over the past ten years to 93,000 annually. Of particular concern is the increase in the use of crack cocaine which is linked to a violent sub-culture

involving guns. Internationally, the illegal drugs trade is big business worth an estimated 8 per cent ($400 billion) of total international trade, rivalling oil, gas and world tourism.

Many factors have been linked to drug abuse by young people, including poverty, youth unemployment and low self-esteem, which can make young people more vulnerable to peer pressure and the desire to appear 'cool'. Nor is it a problem confined to the inner cities; drug misuse goes on in rural communities and market towns all over the country.

Meanwhile, the number of young addicts has spiralled in recent years and there are now between 100,000 and 200,000 addicts in the UK. In 1995 over a third of people needing help from drug agencies were under 25. However, young people tend to see specialist drug services as 'not for them' – but for older, hard drug users.

Most young people today do know about the dangers of drug-taking, just as they know about the risks of smoking and HIV infection, but on balance, many of them choose to take the risks.

My name is heroin

A poem written by a young person taking part in the Southmead Project in Bristol.

My name is heroin – call me smack for short,
I entered this country without a passport.
Ever since I've made lots of scum rich,
Some have been murdered and found in a ditch.
I'm more valued than diamonds, more treasured than gold.
Use me just once and you too will be sold.
I'll take a renowned speaker and make him a bore.
I'll take your mother and make her a whore.
I'll take all your rent money and you'll be evicted,
I'll murder your babies or they'll be born addicted.
I'll make you rob and steal and kill,
When under my power you have no will.
Once I take charge you won't have a prayer,
I make shooting and stabbing a common affair.
Listen to me and please listen well –
When you ride with heroin you are heading for hell.

Peer education: giving young people a voice

Interest in finding alternatives to traditional drugs, smoking and sex education has been growing in recent years, with the concept of peer education coming to the fore.

Young people often have more credibility than adults when it comes to discussing drugs, and their peers will listen more carefully to someone of their own age group who may have 'been there, done that'.

Fast Forward, an Edinburgh-based national voluntary organisation, promotes innovative health education for young people. The project mainly focuses on drugs, providing information about the social, legal and health consequences of drug taking.

'We are not there to find out if people are taking drugs,' says one peer educator with Fast Forward. 'We are trying to get them to think of things they haven't considered before. We don't say "don't". Instead we say "think through the options and look after yourself".'

Fast Forward's peer educators have worked with groups in care homes and clubs as well as comprehensive schools, and new recruits go out with more experienced educators before they go solo. The idea is to give information, rather than advice, and if young people want individual help they are referred on to specialist counsellors.

Agenda for action

What can policy makers, voluntary and statutory agencies do to make a difference?

Smoking
- ban cigarette advertising;
- increase the cost of smoking;
- restrict smoking in public places;
- education campaigns which depict cigarette manufacturers as manipulative and deceitful are more effective than those which point out the dangers to health; and
- discourage adults from smoking, especially in front of children. In an HEA survey of schoolchildren, 66 per cent said that at least one member of their household smoked, compared with 39 per cent of those who never smoked.

Alcohol
Not only adults and parents, but retailers, bar staff and manufacturers have a role to play in tackling teenage alcohol misuse.
- the best way to predict whether a young person is going to have a drink problem is to ask whether his or her parents are heavy drinkers;
- the less that alcohol costs, the more people drink – yet the price of alcohol has been going down for some time; and
- we need restrictions on the marketing of alcohol and alcopops to young people, together with new measures to stop under-18s buying alcohol.

Accidents
- accident prevention has been recognised as a policy issue in the Health of the Nation, which calls for a 33 per cent reduction in deaths for under-15s and 25 per cent reduction for 15 to 24-year-olds; and
- improved safety arrangements in nightclubs.

Mental health
Research identifies various factors which can protect young people from mental health problems, including:
- self-esteem;
- social contact;
- autonomy;
- family warmth and support;
- parents who get on well;
- social networks which encourage young people to cope;
- more support for families; and
- more resources for organisations which support young people.

Drugs
While the long-term 'answers' to Britain's drugs problems are highly contentious and political, certain practical measures are clearly helpful:
- new services for young drug misusers and their families, including programmes to divert young users from custody into treatment and to rebuild relationships;
- a national enquiry into the effectiveness of the existing legal

framework for, and educational policies on, the misuse of drugs;
- Ofsted (*Drug Education in Schools*, 1997) recommends that 'schools do their utmost to avoid using exclusions to deal with drug related incidents. It should be recognised that exclusion can place the pupil at risk of further exposure to drugs';
- Ofsted (as above) considers that schools should plan drugs education for all pupils, and should monitor and assess its effectiveness; and
- in addition to drugs education in schools, young people respond well to education in more informal settings, such as youth work.

Resources and Contacts

Resources

Action, a magazine published by The Prince's Trust.

A Second Chance: Developing mentoring and education projects for young people, by Sarah Benioff, with Dalston Youth Project and Crime Concern. Published by Commission for Racial Equality and Crime Concern, 1997.

Alcohol Concern, Factsheet no. 7. Alcohol Concern.

The Carnegie Young People Initiative: Years of Decision, The Carnegie UK Trust. Youth Work Press, 1996.

The Chemistry Between Us, by Jay Rayner. A feature in *Deluxe* Magazine, spring 1998.

The Education of Children Who Are Looked After by Local Authorities, Ofsted.

General Household Survey

Key Data on Adolescence, by John Coleman. Trust for the Study of Adolescence, 1997.

Leaving Home, by Gill Jones. Open University Press, 1995.

Misspent Youth ... Young People and Crime, The Audit Commission, 1996.

National Survey of Sexual Attitudes and Lifestyles, by Kaye Wellings et al. Penguin, 1994.

Ofsted Annual Report, 1997.

Preventative Strategy for Young People in Trouble, a report by Coopers & Lybrand, commissioned by ITV Telethon/The Prince's Trust, 1994.

Sexual Health, Health Education Authority, 1997.

Speaking Up, Speaking Out! The 2020 Vision Programme Summary Research Report, The Industrial Society, 1997.

Strides, a practical guide to sexual relationships education with young men, by Simon Blake and Joanna Laxton. Family Planning Association.

Understanding and Working with Young Women in Custody. Training pack by HM Prison Service and the Trust for the Study of Adolescence, 1996.

Violent Victims: the prevalence of abuse and loss in the lives of Section 53 offenders, by Dr Gwyneth Boswell. The Prince's Trust and the Royal Jubilee Trusts, 1995.

Young People, Alcohol and their Social World, Health Education Authority, 1998.

Young People Now, a monthly magazine by the National Youth Agency.

Young People and Crime in Scotland; A Report by The Prince's Trust–Action, The Prince's Trust, 1997.

Young People and Health: the health behaviour of school-aged children, Health Education Authority, 1997.

Young Prisoners; A Thematic Review, HM Inspector of Prisons, 1997.

Youth, the Underclass and Social Exclusion, edited by Robert MacDonald. Routledge, 1997.

Contacts

ChildLine,
Freepost 111,
London N1 0BR.
Tel: 0800 1111.

Commission for Racial Equality,
Elliot House,
10–12 Allington Street,
London SW1E 5EH.
Tel: 0171 828 7022.

Crime Concern,
Signal Point,
Station Road,
Swindon SN1 1FE.
Tel: 01793 514596. Fax: 01793 514654.

Dalston Youth Project,
The Round Chapel,
Powerscroft Road,
Lower Clapton,
London E5 OLY.
Tel: 0181 525 9696. Fax: 0181 525 9394.

DIVERT (the national charity for the prevention of youth crime),
32 King Street,
Covent Garden,
London WC2E 8JD.
Tel: 0171 379 6171. Fax: 0171 240 2082.

Family Planning Association,
2–12 Pentonville Road,
London N1 9FP.
Tel: 0171 837 5432.

Health Education Authority
Trevelyan House,
30 Great Peter Street,
London SW1P 2HW
Tel: 0171 222 5300.
(Including the **Young People and Schools Programme**)

NACRO,
National Asociation for the Care and Resettlement of Offenders,
169 Clapham Road,
London SW9 OPU.
Tel: 0171 582 6500. Fax: 0171 735 4666.

National Children's Bureau,
8 Wakley Street,
London EC1V 7QE.
Tel: 0171 843 6000.
(Also, the **Sex Education Forum**)

QUIT,

102 Gloucester Place,

London W1H 3DA.

Tel: 0171 487 2858.

The National Youth Agency,

17–23 Albion Street,

Leicester LE1 6GD.

Tel: 0116 285 6789. Fax: 0116 247 1043.

The Prince's Trust,

18 Park Square East,

London NW1 4LH.

Tel: 0171 543 1234. Fax: 0171 543 1200.

The Trust for the Study of Adolescence,

23 New Road,

Brighton,

East Sussex BN1 1WZ

Tel: 01237 693311. Fax: 01273 679907.

The Unemployment Unit and Youthaid,

322 St John Street,

London EC1V 4NT.

Tel: 0171 833 8499.